Praise for the *Earth Spirit* series

There is no doubt that this world is in crisis. The ecological and sociological reality we're living in and must face up to is quite frankly terrifying. Yet there is hope. The authors of the *Earth Spirit* series from Moon Books show us that there are solutions to be found in ecological and eco-spiritual practices. I recommend this series to anyone who is concerned about our current situation and wants to find some hope in solutions they can practice for themselves.
Sarah Kerr, Pagan Federation President

This bold and rich *Earth Spirit* series provides vital information, perspectives, poetry and wisdom to guide and support through the complex environmental, climate and biodiversity challenges and crisis facing us all. Nothing is avoided within the wide range of author views, expertise and recommendations on eco-spirituality. I am deeply inspired by the common call, across the books, to radically change our relationship with the planet to a more respectful, mutual, spiritual and sustainable way of living; both individually and collectively. Each book offers its own particular flavour and practical offering of solutions and ways forward in these unprecedented times. Collectively the series provides an innovative, inspiring and compelling compendium of how to live, hope and act from both ancient and modern wisdoms. Whatever your views, concerns and aspirations for your life, and for the planet, you will find something of value. My life and understanding is deeply enhanced through the privilege of reading this series.
Dr Lynne Sedgmore CBE, Founder of Goddess Luminary Leadership Wheel, Executive Coach, F
Executive

In a world that is faced with such immense environmental issues, we can often feel paralysed and impotent. The *Earth Spirit* series is a welcome and inspiring antidote to fear and apathy. These books gift us with positive and inspiring visions that serve to empower and strengthen our own resolve to contribute to the healing of our planet, our communities and ourselves.

Eimear Burke, Chosen Chief of The Order of Bards, Ovates and Druids

Thanks to Moon Books and an amazing group of authors for stepping up in support of our need to address, with grace and aliveness, the ecological crises facing humanity. We must take concerted, focused, positive action on every front NOW, and this is best and most powerfully done when we base our offerings in a deep sense of spirit. White Buffalo Woman came to us 20 generations ago, reminding us of the importance of a holy perception of the world - based in Oneness, unity, honor and respect. Even as that is profound, it is also practical, giving us a baseline of power from which to give our gifts of stewardship and make our Earth walk a sacred one - for us and for All Our Relations. Walk in Beauty with these authors!

Brooke Medicine Eagle, Earthkeeper and author of *Buffalo Woman Comes Singing* and *The Last Ghost Dance*

Earth Spirit is an exciting and timely series. It has never been more important to engage with ideas that promote a positive move forward for our world. Our planet needs books like these - they offer us heartening signposts through the most challenging of times.

Philip Carr-Gomm, author of *Druid Mysteries, Druidcraft* and *Lessons in Magic*

Our relationship to the Mother Earth and remembering our roles as caretakers and guardians of this sacred planet is essential in weaving ourselves back into the tapestry of our own sacred nature. From the shamanic perspective, we are not separate from nature. The journey to finding solutions for the Earth will come through each person's reconnection to her heartbeat and life force.

Chandra Sun Eagle, author of *Looking Back on the Future*

This is important work as we humans face one of the greatest challenges in our collective history.

Ellen Evert Hopman, Archdruid of Tribe of the Oak and author of *A Legacy of Druids, A Druid's Herbal of Sacred Tree Medicine, The Sacred Herbs of Spring*, and other volumes

EARTH SPIRIT

Beyond Sustainability

Authentic Living at a
Time of Climate Crisis

EARTH SPIRIT

Beyond Sustainability

Authentic Living at a Time of Climate Crisis

Nimue Brown

MOON
BOOKS

Winchester, UK
Washington, USA

JOHN HUNT PUBLISHING

First published by Moon Books, 2023
Moon Books is an imprint of John Hunt Publishing Ltd., No. 3 East Street, Alresford
Hampshire SO24 9EE, UK
office@jhpbooks.net
www.johnhuntpublishing.com
www.moon-books.net

For distributor details and how to order please visit the 'Ordering' section on our website.

Design: Matthew Greenfield

UK: Printed and bound by CPI Group (UK) Ltd, Croydon, CR0 4YY
Printed in North America by CPI GPS partners

We operate a distinctive and ethical publishing philosophy in
all areas of our business, from our global network of authors to
production and worldwide distribution.

Contents

For Trevor Greenfield

Introduction

What do we really want from life? How do we find happiness, health, purpose and comfort? Humans are increasingly a miserable species, caught in ways of behaving that give us very little and will cost us the Earth.

While we're convinced that saving what remains of life on the planet would cost us too much, we won't do it. We need to think seriously about what it means to be human, what it means to live, and how much we stand to lose.

With this book, I hope to show you how much we stand to gain from abandoning capitalism. Life could be good. We could have rich, peaceful and joyful lives. All we'd really have to give up is our misery and competitiveness.

What if it was easy to change our lives? What if happiness wasn't an impossible dream to chase after? What if we could have nice things? The answer is simple. The answer begins with authenticity.

Chapter 1

What Makes an Authentic Life?

What does it mean to live in an authentic way? This is a question that has been central to my path as a Druid for many years now, and it is primarily through Druidry that I have found my answers. I have written this book from an intrinsically Druidic perspective, but without assumption about who you are or what path you are on when you read this. Authenticity is not the sole preserve of Druidry and can be sought through any sincere exploration of life and self.

For me, the authentic life is the consciously chosen life. It's what we do when we make our most informed and most deliberate choices. Our most authentic responses to life aren't the unconsidered, knee-jerk reactions occurring in the moment. Authenticity isn't acting on autopilot or playing out stories held by our societies. When we don't know why we're doing what we're doing we are most likely to be playing out the stories of our families and cultures and being led by whatever we've unconsciously absorbed. Your most authentic self is the person you truly want to be and are working to become.

Following a spiritual path is a choice based on the desire to discover and become our most authentic self. The same is true when we approach life philosophically. We quest after meaning and purpose, we seek guidance, values and insight so as to live well. For the Pagan, spirituality and sustainability are intertwined. To honour the Earth as sacred, you have to live out that commitment in your daily life. Thus it seems to me that to live authentically as a Pagan must also mean to live sustainably.

The things that support physical and mental health in humans are also invariably better choices for the health of the planet as a whole. Industrialised, capitalist living has distorted our sense

2

of what's good for us. However, the answer is not to daydream about going back to some sort of fantasy-history. What we need are the changes we can make right now in our own lives.

I know there are a lot of people who see the move towards sustainability as a life-denying choice. I see a lot of that kind of thinking from right wing commentators. The sense of having to give up, go without, move backwards, abandon progress and all the rest of it doesn't seem appealing. Why would it? But this is just a story designed to keep us where we are doing what we always do. It's a path that makes most of us ill and miserable, and is costing us the Earth.

I am excited about the kinds of changes that make life more sustainable. I've been exploring those changes on a personal level for some time, and writing about my experiences on my Druidlife blog. The deeper I go with this quest for a more sustainable way of living, the happier I am in myself and the more rewarding I find my life. Let me assure you, however, that this isn't smug privilege masquerading as sustainability. Mine is a low income household, we have a number of challenges and I wrangle continually with an abuse legacy that has caused me considerable psychological damage and a body that doesn't work that well.

Sustainable living that reduces the impact of climate change moves us towards better ways of living. Many of those improvements can offer most to those who have least. I'm prepared to ask people who can afford such outrageous things to give up their cruises and their private jets so that other people do not watch their homes disappear under water.

Not everyone will be able to do everything I suggest in this book. My hope is to give you ways of thinking about your life and your aspirations that will set you on a path to greater authenticity, greater joy and a more viable way of existing. For some changes to be possible, we will need political involvement, and I will talk about that, although it isn't the main focus of this work.

Conscious Living

Conscious living is the key to many doors. It puts us much more in charge of our feelings, choices and lives. The more we pay attention to life, the more informed our decisions and actions are. The flip side of this is that if you are running around frantically, time poor, under pressure, constantly busy and with no time to reflect, then you barely know what you're doing and are easy to manipulate. When you're desperately time poor, you are obliged to buy whatever solutions and comforts you can and there's no scope to consider the costs or the alternatives.

Many people struggle to meditate because they can't shut down the noise in their own minds to achieve inner quiet. Faced with late stage capitalism and climate chaos, I don't think the answer is to try and shut down that inner noise. We need instead to pay close attention to it.

Make time every day to just sit down and spend time with yourself. If you are time poor, then just a few minutes is enough to start making change. Ideally, you should take as much time as you need, but that may not be possible. If you think better with something in your hands, you can do this while doodling, crafting or doing housework. Pay attention to your thoughts as they arise, but don't dismiss them, find out what they are. What are you worrying about? What are you trying to figure out? What needs your attention?

If anything seems especially large, complex or important, try writing it down so that you can return to it. Find out about the needs, feelings and issues that are most important to you. Start making time for dealing with that, and don't drown it out with distractions. Some of what emerges will likely be grief and distress around climate chaos, habitat loss and extinction. You don't have to process all of that in one go, and it is hard to face. We can't live authentically and be in denial about the anguish of human destructiveness.

When you make time for your thoughts and feelings in this

way, they will start to clarify. You'll know what's bothering you, and what's crying out for attention. You will become more alert to your own discomfort and in the short term this is an unpleasant process. Most of us are not living in ways that support and nurture us. Facing up to that is painful. Meanwhile, our culture keeps offering to sell us more distractions, more noise, more ways to blot out the inadequacy we might otherwise feel. Becoming conscious of all of this can be painful and depressing, but it is a necessary first step towards making radical change and moving towards happiness and fulfilment.

Conscious living means making time for the right things. It means knowing what you need and what nourishes and fulfils you. While the details of this will be personal, there are some broad areas where we tend to be much alike.

There is a suggestion out there that if you feel you can't meditate for half an hour every day, you should meditate for an hour. This is a cruel and useless thought. Take what time you can. Carving out space for your own thoughts and feelings takes time. Showing up for a few minutes when you can, is a good way to get started.

Authentic Relationships

Humans are social mammals. We tend to be happiest when we feel seen, respected, understood and valued by other humans. We crave relationships with other humans, and we do best when those relationships are based on cooperation and sharing rather than competition and jealousy. Working together, playing together, celebrating and enriching each other's lives, we have considerable scope for finding joy, purpose and reward through our relationships with each other. We have the most power to make meaningful change when we work together.

Capitalist culture teaches us to compete, to hoard whatever seems scarce, to be possessive, jealous, mistrustful and resentful. We tell each other that there must be winners and losers, that our win is confirmed by someone else's loss and our social value is about having more stuff than other people. This is a joyless way to live and it is utterly toxic to the planet.

If instead we prioritised fair sharing, meeting people's needs, creating justice, and if we rejected economic 'valuing' of people, we'd all be a lot happier. If you dedicate your life to keeping up with the neighbours, or trying to get ahead of your nearest and dearest, the victories are all dependent on someone else failing. When we see winning is a collective goal, we can all win and it's a much happier and more sustainable way to live.

We have the material resources to take care of everyone. There is no need for hunger, for homelessness, for abject poverty. There is no need for anyone to live in misery. These are political choices, and the consequences of our many individual choices. There's also nothing inevitable about inequality, poverty or desperation, it's just a consequence of the system we've chosen to adopt.

Authentic Presence

What would it take for you to feel truly authentic? How much time and energy do you spend on pretending to be someone you are not? How much of that pretence is an economic necessity? How much of it is a consequence of social pressure? Who would you be and how would you live if you were able to truly live an authentic life?

How much of your sense of self is informed by money? How much of your personhood is defined by your job, or by not being in work, or not being able to work? How meaningful is your work to you? What would happen to your sense of self if your economic situation changed? To what degree is your sense of self informed by your spending power and by the display of your wealth and possessions? Are your brand preferences part of your identity? How much of your personhood has been sold to you through advertising? To what degree are you simply a product of your background?

When we don't have time for reflection, we can end up having our identities sold to us as consumers. Who you are becomes where you shop, the clothes you buy, whose labels you wear, or which soft drinks you favour. There's no room for an authentic sense of self if your identity is being sold to you.

How much of the desire to over-consume comes from the pressure to construct our identities out of products? How much do we consume because we don't want to look poor, or out of date, or unfashionable, or irrelevant? Advertising is designed to play on our fears and to offer us solutions to problems that have been invented to sell us stuff in the first place. So we spend money we can't really afford to have things we don't need in order to feel socially engaged and relevant. All that desire for love, respect and a place in our communities – those basic and ancient human urges – are so easily co-opted to make us into relentless consumers. The business strategies that are driving the climate crisis also rob us of our scope for peaceful, authentic living.

The woods do not care what you are wearing. The sky is not interested in your bank balance. The wild things are unimpressed by your gadgets. Out on the hills, in the fields and on the riverbanks, or in whatever open space surrounds you, your consumer identity is meaningless. It is good to get outside consciously and to feel the elements with your body while reminding yourself that consumer culture has no pertinence here. Be scruffy. Wear old clothes. Hold no technology in your hands. Nature is indifferent to all of those things.

Now imagine what it would be like to move in human circles where the relentless pressure to purchase didn't exist. Picture the friends who aren't excited about brands, influencers, fashion or the latest must-have. Imagine the people who want you for your own sake and who are impressed by your ideas, your kindness, your effort. Imagine feeling that your face and body

7

are good enough and do not require endless modification with products. Perhaps you are wise or lucky enough to have already found such spaces and attracted such friends. Trying to impress people with your consumerism is never-ending and exhausting. It's not a winnable game and it will never reward you. Today's shiny new proof that you are ahead is tomorrow's evidence that you have already fallen behind. We don't have to live like this, and freeing ourselves from this relentless and merciless process makes room for much more actual joy. Sustainable pleasures are a lot more enduring, and don't come with the constant threat of failure around not keeping up.

True Nourishment and Fulfilment

What feeds your soul? What inspires you and uplifts you? What in your life brings you true joy and satisfaction? To know yourself is to also know what brings you fulfilment. If our lives are too full of white noise, frenetic action and overstimulation then we don't get to really explore these questions. Consumer culture is good at selling us the idea of things that will fulfil us. Tragically, at the same time we're constantly sold messages of dissatisfaction to keep us consuming. We're not allowed to relish what we already own, or who we are, or what we do. We have to be quickly persuaded that what we've got isn't good enough so that we'll buy something new.

Satisfaction isn't something we can purchase. A fulfilling life isn't about owning the right things. Once our basic needs are met, we don't get much extra happiness from having more wealth and material goods. In fact, those things can increase our anxiety and insecurity. If our needs are met, our happiness is more likely found in being able to enjoy what we have.

Part of the problem with throwaway culture is that we have no relationships with objects. There's no love for possessions when everything is destined for landfill soon anyway. When what we own has been lovingly made or thoughtfully chosen and we mean to have that item be part of our lives for years to come, there's a lot more scope for valuing, enjoyment and appreciation. Throwaway culture denies us joy and meaning. Meanwhile it turns valuable resources into problematic waste and pumps carbon into the atmosphere. It takes a great deal from us and gives us low quality things in return, and empty promises. Further, the things that need constantly replacing usually cost more money than the things we can keep using. We pay more for less benefit, and the cost to the planet is vast and inexcusable.

It's hard to look for fulfilment when we're constantly distracted by attractive, unsatisfying things. It can be hard even to admit that we aren't happy when we're surrounded by messages about how consumption is supposed to make us feel good. Depression is a widespread condition. Loneliness is so common. We're told that retail therapy is the answer, when trying to buy our way to happiness is actually the problem.

Genuine happiness comes from self-respect and from finding our lives inherently meaningful and rewarding. We are nourished by things that stimulate our minds, bring good sensations to our bodies and that enrich us emotionally. We need hope and wonder, beauty and delight. We need opportunities to do things that mean we can like and respect ourselves as people. We need meaningful relationships with each other, with the land and with our immediate surroundings. We cannot consume our way into significance.

Chapter 2

Authenticity and the Unsustainable

We are a mammal species that has evolved to live on one specific planet. Everything about us has been shaped by the world we live in. How could we possibly imagine that living in ways that damage our home is in any way reasonable or desirable? And yet here we are, obsessed with consumption and material wealth, and trying to control nature even as we create disasters. Authenticity and viability alike depend on us learning to live within our means.

White, northern hemisphere humans have a lot of stories about how we are separate from and superior to nature. Those stories are killing us and killing the planet. We are just one creature among many, no more entitled to exist than any other. Nature does not exist to serve us. We are not entitled to dominion over all things, and we most assuredly are not entitled to destroy other species in the name of our dominion. We need new stories, and we also need to examine the stories we tell each other, and what those stories actually do to us.

The story is that we have trickle-down economics where the wealthy create jobs and quality of life for the majority. The reality is that the wealth gap is getting bigger. Capitalism exploits workers, paying them less than their time and output is really worth. The Earth is exploited for resources with no recognition of the cost. The consumer is then asked to pay more than the product is worth. The difference between what the consumer pays and what the worker is paid creates profit for shareholders. All of this depends on us keeping on working and buying and using more than the planet can bear.

To make matters worse, our governments have decided that growth is the best measure of everything, that growth is desirable, and that our economies shall be based upon it. This means that we all have to work more, make more stuff, consume more stuff and spend more money, always and forever. With finite resources, this clearly isn't possible. We're operating on the basis of a story that demonstrably cannot be true or feasible.

Here's an example. The further you go back in history, the slower clothing fashions were to change. When I was a child, fashion was seasonal, so you might be looking at new fashions each quarter, if you were really keen. Fashion is now weekly for those who are serious about it, and many people buy things to wear once and then throw them away. We can only have growth in the fashion industry if we become more willing to buy new clothes more often. How much faster can we go? Do we need daily fashion? Hourly? Where does it stop? What's the psychological cost of trying to keep up with this? In order to have growth in the fashion industry we have to have ever more consumption and waste – manifestly this isn't viable.

We are told stories that engage us as consumers. We are subject to those stories every day, through advertisements. These advertisements are designed specifically to get into our heads and inform our feelings and choices. Advertisements are designed to manipulate us in order to make us consume – and they work. We've bought a lot of unsustainable ideas alongside the products we've been persuaded that we need.

The stories informing our lives tell us that new is better than old. Having new things makes us look important, informed and worthy of respect. If we do not have new things people may think we are poor or ignorant. We may be left behind and not know what's going on or what is important. We may be seen to have been left behind and we should fear the social stigma associated with that. No one will respect us if we do not have the right shiny new things. It is important to replace things when they are out of date – not because they are broken or worn out. Being professional means looking a certain way. A nice home means regular dousing with chemicals – everything must sparkle and must smell of synthetic perfumes at all times. Dirt is a moral failing so we must look spotless at all times. Cars make us free. Sofas make us happy. Deodorants are how we find love. Relationships are about having the right food in your very new and shiny fridge. And on it goes.

We are bombarded with these stories all the time. Without the space for peaceful reflection, we might not even notice how relentless these stories are and how they impact on us emotionally. Nothing we buy will ever be allowed to be good enough for long.

For growth to be possible, we have to replace things at ever greater speeds, and we have to expand our populations so that there are ever more people to be workers and consumers. We call consumerist countries 'developed'. We call countries where people are living closer to the land 'developing' or 'under-developed' – I find this language use really sinister. But growth requires new markets, new consumers, new demand. We're already using more than the planet can bear, but to keep on growing we'd have to expand current consumption. It is manifestly insane and suicidal.

Spending money can give us fleeting feelings of power and control over our lives. We buy things that may please or comfort us in the short term, but we do not become happy as a consequence. We buy our dissatisfaction at the same time and are unable to escape from it within this system. For as long as we believe that we can buy our way to happiness and that consumption is the answer, we are doomed to personal misery and planetary crisis.

We need new stories, and we need to debunk the stories that we're currently living in. Consumption does not make us happy. Brands do not give us meaningful identities. We cannot keep going faster all the time. New things are not always better. High speed living and 24/7 culture is exhausting. Aspiring to own a bigger fridge or a new sofa is not the kind of dream that sustains anyone emotionally. Cars have us sitting in traffic queues breathing in poison – they do not equate to freedom. We have to debunk these stories on the way to coming up with something better.

High Speed Living

In theory it's exciting to live in the fast lane. You're busy! You're important! You're going somewhere! But there's never time to ask where the fast lane is taking us or what we're missing as we dash headlong towards another day of headlong dashing. Life on the go, the busy, modern urban lifestyle, the kind of life where you have to grab things to keep going – we are normalised to all of this through adverts and lifestyle content. How many of us have simply absorbed the idea that being on the go all the time is necessary and unavoidable? Meanwhile, workplaces capitalise on this, expecting emails to be answered at all hours, eroding boundaries around time off and demanding more for less.

Not only is it hard to stop or slow down, it may be terrifying. How many people are actually crawling through life in a state of overload and exhaustion, not actually going anywhere, but trapped in the illusion of speed?

As a self-employed person I've been able to test some of this extensively over many years. Here is what I've learned. Exhaustion makes you slow and inefficient. Burn out leads to poor decision making, inefficiency and minimal motivation. Being stressed doesn't result in doing good work. Time off, including shorter working days and shorter working weeks radically increases productivity. If I aim to work less, I will reliably achieve more. But when we're exhausted, as workers we are much less discriminating as consumers and it's all part of the same problem.

We'd do far less harm to the planet if we worked and consumed less. This would be easily achieved if the aim was to do the best quality work and have the best quality things. For that to happen we'd have to let go of the idea that spending a lot of time working is itself meaningful and virtuous. We'd have to let go of the macho aspect of work culture where sacrificing yourself for your job is presented as a good thing. We would also have to collectively agree to stop treating rest as a luxury. If we did what was good or necessary and used what we needed, consumption would decrease and with it, carbon emissions. We could have economies based on quality of life rather than growth and making rubbish, but we'd have to stop treating growth itself as a valuable thing.

Imagine how workplaces would change if we didn't have our current stories about what we need to wear to look professional. Imagine life without the roads clogged with commuters, and without the monumental waste of time, energy and carbon that relentless commuting causes. Imagine working less and living more. What would it be like if life didn't revolve around work?

Right now, some of us have more power to change how we work than others. If you have options, consider them. Take a look at what your working life costs you, and what it costs the planet. Consider what you ask of other people when dealing with them professionally. If you are an employer, think about the kind of work culture you create.

Of course, high speed living isn't just about work. It's about having exciting leisure time where you jet around the world, party all night in brightly lit cities, go on adventures and enjoy amazing luxuries. In practice, it isn't like that for most of us, and instead we end up buying things that symbolise our desire to be seen as the sort of person who does that. How many people buy four by four vehicles because they wish to be seen as outdoorsy and active? How many garages contain things bought by people who wanted a lifestyle, but ended up with a product? Surfboards and gym equipment, and gear for hobbies that no one has time or energy for.

If that one doesn't trap you, it'll instead be the feeling that you should be doing better. This might mean having a second job, or a side hustle. You should make your hobby pay money. You should do your hobby to a professional standard. Your spare time should be spent on self-improvement – fitness, beauty, education. If you don't feel you can have fun you might be persuaded to consume self-improvement products instead. For a lot of people, that's just another type of consumption that doesn't do for you what it claimed it would. The more miserable you are, the more likely you are to try and console yourself with products.

Doing less can take some planning. It can feel vulnerable to lower your standards or give up on some ambitions. Take the time to ask what you're chasing and aspiring to – it probably isn't realistic. One good way to claim back some of your time and energy while benefiting the planet, is to do less cleaning. Our cleaning products aren't good for us, or for anything else. Wash things a little less often – including your own body. Stop judging your home by the impossible standards in adverts, and let things go a little. Be gentle with yourself and make a little time to do nothing.

Cleaning products introduce chemicals to your home. We actually benefit from much of the bacteria in our environments. There is friendly bacteria on our skin and in our guts, and it is best not to kill it! Consider what we add to the water with our 'cleaning' and how much water we use for cleaning. Consider the energy use involved with vacuum cleaners, washing machines, dishwashers, tumble driers. Cleaning products often come in single use plastic containers. How much of our time could we free up by settling for 'good enough? How much environmental damage could we avoid if we stopped trying to make our living spaces resemble the spaces we see in the media?

There's an art to doing nothing. I favour gazing out of the window and watching the world go by. However you approach

15

it, the key things are to let your body truly rest, and to let your mind wander. This way you get time to process your thoughts and feelings. Humans are the only mammals that rush around all the time – it is in the nature of mammals to rest. Resting is good for us, it restores us and gives us better health. When we're not really doing anything, we aren't consuming anything either. The less time we spend consuming, the more natural we get to be and the less harm we do.

We're under so much pressure to be active and to consume that resisting can be difficult. It helps to do this with other people so that you feel supported in doing it. Given how much of our social identities can be based in work and consumption, slowing down may feel like losing yourself. However, slowing down gives us far more than it takes away.

Debt Culture

We're so used to debt. Buy now, pay later. Even when we're just talking about money, there's a hidden cost that we seldom appreciate. The interest on our debts means that we pay far more for things we buy in this way than we would if we could just buy them outright. Being poor can be really expensive for just this reason.

We are encouraged to live beyond our means. We buy things we can't afford and we pay it off, or we fail to do that. Debts are sold on as assets, which is even more problematic. Student debt is normal. In America, medical debt destroys lives.

As a species, we're living beyond our means. We're so used to this as an idea that it doesn't terrify us anything like as much as it should. As a planet, we can't declare bankruptcy and move on. We can't keep shuffling the debt by moving it to a new, interest free credit card for the next six months.

Living in debt, and taking more than is sustainable are not authentic ways of living. Personal debt isn't always the choice of the individual and it isn't always about making poor choices. To buy a home, deal with medical problems or have an education, creates debt for people around the world. This is something we'd need political action to change. Life should not be based on debt in this way.

In terms of our life on this planet, debt isn't an option. We must learn to live within our means. We have to understand our limits – how much carbon we can afford, how much water we can use, how much land actually exists... and we have to keep humanity within those boundaries. *Doughnut Economics* by Kate Raworth has a lot to offer on this subject.

Unconscious Living

If you aren't consciously making choices about your life, who is deciding how you live? The things we absorb as normal, and that we do not question have tremendous power over us. The person who does not live consciously is at the mercy of adverts, the media, their society and anything at all that they come into contact with where there's an agenda of any sort. It's a terrible way to live, and it denies a person self-knowledge and self-determination.

One of the things high speed living does is to rob us of self-determination. When we spend our time over-stimulated, and moving quickly from one thing to another we can be directed by others and not even realise we aren't in control. Thus we end up impulse buying things and then having no idea why we even wanted them. We end up with debts, clutter, and are ever more dependent on working just to stay afloat.

There are things it is difficult to be conscious of. The human brain isn't very good at handling massive threats that seem like they're a long way off. This certainly isn't helping us at the moment. It takes effort to absorb both the horror and the urgency of the climate disaster unfolding around us. Ignoring what's happening, denying it or just hoping the problems will go away is an understandable human response. We have to resist that, and consciously face up to what's happening, and learn how to do better.

When we're living unconsciously, we are easily persuaded that products are the answer to our unexamined feelings and needs. We're persuaded to go along with whatever seems normal and familiar, no matter what the implications are. Unconscious living makes us willing to be exploited for the benefit of others. We accept endless work and unhappy lives because we've come to believe these things are normal and inevitable. We could be much happier than this.

Materialism and Relationship

When we interact with the material world, we enter into relationships. If those relationships are fleeting, careless and exploitative, that's part of our relationship with the Earth. As Pagans, we should care about those relationships. Everything we own has come from the land. The harm caused by creating things and by disposing of them is part of our relationship with the natural world.

When we bring something home, we are entering into a relationship with where it came from, how it was made and what happens when we are done with it. That relationship includes pollution, carbon footprint, water consumption, habitat loss, and extinction. It might also involve slave labour, child cruelty, violence against indigenous people, or corruption. The products we buy may be helping fund destructive, oppressive politics.

Practically speaking, it's a huge and emotionally exhausting job to understand the implications of every single thing you buy. However, the more aware we are, the better. If we buy things from closer to home, we have a better chance of knowing who we are supporting and what the implications are. Buying second hand reduces the harm caused and doesn't pour money into problematic companies or industries. We can also consider borrowing and sharing as ways of minimising the harm caused by the objects in our lives. Any time and care you invest in this way is an act of dedication to the natural world.

I invite you to take a more animist approach to anything you invite into your home. When we see objects as also being possessed of spirit, it is harder to treat them casually. We can have more meaningful experiences of our possessions when we enter into deliberate relationships with them. If you buy things with the intention of having a relationship, it will help to inform your purchasing choices. It's also a better way to live. Being surrounded by things that have no meaning or value to you does not improve your quality of life. When your home is populated by things that are significant to you and that you intend to have as part of your life for the longer term, those relationships will enrich you.

The more we know about where our food and possessions come from, the more of a relationship we have with the things that are part of our lives. Eating locally grown food can help you form a relationship with the land. Knowing who made the objects around you can give you a relationship with your community. Being with items over a period of years makes them part of your story and your sense of self. Having meaningful relationships with the material world takes us away from throw-away culture. It's better for us, and it's better for the planet. I have a bookcase that belonged to my great grandparents, and various things that belonged to my grandparents. This gives me feelings of connection with my ancestors.

When nothing around us has meaning or intrinsic value, that's really alienating. Having a sense of connection gives us feelings of belonging. If our homes are animist communities and we are amongst friends when in the company of our possessions, this is a less lonely way to live. If what we own connects us to each other, to our communities, friends, landscape and wider home in the Earth, that brings meaning and depth to life.

Brands are increasingly trying to present themselves as

people. A lot of marketing work goes into the idea of persuading you that a brand is something you can have a relationship with, as though it was another person. Should animism extend to the idea that a corporate entity is also an entity? Can we really have a relationship with such an entity, beyond the transactional exchange of money for goods? If we are persuaded to invest emotionally in our relationship with a brand, what do we get in return? Does the brand care for us in a reciprocal way? Or are we just being exploited, and having our need for relationships used against us for the economic gain of people we will never meet?

The more personal an object is, the more scope there is to have a relationship with it, or through it to have relationships with people, landscapes and more. When we buy mass-produced things from brands we're still in relationships with where it all came from and how it was made, but we have little scope for that relationship to be visible to us, and we don't get much of a say in it. The relationship itself is not balanced or equitable.

When we source things from people, from small companies or endeavours local to us, there's much more scope for involvement. The act of buying from a maker or a smaller company has a much bigger impact on them, too. A big chain store or a large corporation barely notices what you spend. A small producer is much more affected by you buying from them. If you are interested in expressing identity or values through economic choices, then buying from small producers does far more good than picking a brand.

When we make, repair, upcycle and receive objects as gifts, they can become more meaningful to us. When we become part of an object's history, we are powerful and effective people in relation to that item. If your home contains things you made, salvaged or had custom made, what they reflect back to you is much more interesting than anything you will get from a regular, mass produced item.

The material culture we choose does have a big impact on us.

Our sense of who we are is shaped by our environments, and we often get to choose those environments. If our surroundings are full of things that hold no meaning for us, that has considerable implications. If we choose beauty, significance and a reflection of our values, then our surroundings will help us feel better about ourselves. We do choose who we are when we are able to make shopping choices, but adverts lie to us about what those choices mean and what is likely to give us most.

Consumption as Balm

For every problem we have, there's a solution we can buy. We're constantly shown that family unity is about buying the right things. Looking for love? Buy things. Lonely? You need the right products to make people like you. Many of us live lonely, isolated lives while being told that individualism is good and that paying for things is going to make us feel better.

Once our basic material needs are met, spending more money doesn't do much to make us happier. If we really did go the whole distance with product ownership shaping our relationships, could anyone truly be happy in that sort of situation? How bland would we have to be if we could find our family unity in the right kind of gravy? How much would you trust a lover you really believed you had seduced with the power of your perfume? Mass produced products do not give us real relationships with other people.

In my experience, relationships are most substantial when founded in shared activity. People who do stuff together tend to build stronger and more enduring relationships. By this I don't mean simply consuming the same stuff together. Active sharing and participation is really key. When you get groups of people who turn up in each other's lives for multiple reasons, then you start to get feelings of community and mutual involvement.

Buying solutions is at odds with this. Cooking together is more of a bonding experience than going out for a meal.

Making a quilt together is a bonding experience, buying a duvet isn't. Meeting to sing and tell stories is a bonding experience, subscribing to Netflix isn't. Our ancestors mostly couldn't buy solutions and dealt with many of their challenges by working together. The quilting and storytelling are just two examples of the kinds of things people used to do as communities and that now we just buy. What we gain in speed and ease we often lose in involvement and depth.

Dealing with people can be hard work, and it can be fraught with problems. Buying a product so often looks like a quick and easy option. Negotiating with other people to find a solution can be slow and frustrating. But people need people in ways that product-based solutions can't offer. We need to share our lives and experiences with other people, and we need to exist in a social context. It would be difficult for most of us to live an authentic and meaningful life without other people being an active part of it.

We're so used to thinking of our challenges as personal problems for which we must find or buy our own solutions. When we seek collective solutions, everything changes. There is so much that can be done through sharing, mutual aid and being community minded. When those who have resources step up to help those who are struggling, all kinds of solutions become possible. Further, when we find community solutions, we get the opportunity to be valued and respected, to feel cared for and supported – all of which is rewarding and nourishing.

Marketing Your Dreams

What do you daydream about? What do you long for? For your life to be complete, what would you need? If your responses were mostly about things you want to own, then your dreams have been invaded by marketing. It's not an accident – this is what marketing exists to do. If you aren't persuaded you need something, why would you buy it? I've worked in marketing, and have studied it. I can say with some confidence that the purpose of marketing is usually to get you to want things you don't actually want.

While the desire for experiences can be more environmentally friendly than the desire for possessions, this too gets co-opted by adverts. If the experience requires you to get on an aeroplane, or a cruise ship, or otherwise spend a lot of money, it's still primarily a form of consumption. There is no marketing department selling you the idea of friendship without consumerism. You are not routinely hearing messages about the benefits of not doing much, giving things away, sharing resources or getting more sleep. There are many things that are good for us, and good for the planet that aren't being advocated for because they don't make a profit for someone.

Reclaiming your dreams is excellent work to be doing if you want a more authentic and sustainable life. Taking the time to investigate your desires will help you identify the degree to which your current dreams have been hijacked by people trying to sell you stuff. Noticing what you long for can help you free yourself from the pressures created by people who are just selling you something. Consider the ways in which you feel dissatisfied with your life as it currently is, and look for the ways in which that dissatisfaction may have been sold to you in the first place, to soften you up as a consumer.

What do you really want? It should be the most personal of questions, resulting in answers that are yours and only yours. Do your dreams look like a one size fits all sale rail? If they do, then ask what part of your true self has been co-opted by consumerism.

The desire to own domestic things – dining table, sofa, kitchen gadgets – can be about the desire to have a happy and harmonious family life, or the kind of social life where people share food. It's not really about the objects at all. The objects are not an answer to difficulties or insufficiencies and they aren't

23

what make human relationships work.

Clothes, fashion, gyms, exercise equipment, beauty products... these are all often pitched to us in ways that make us feel inadequate and unlovable. The implicit promise is that with the right possessions, we become loveable. Of course, we want to be loved, we may want to be desired. What we want are relationships that affirm us and make us feel good about ourselves.

Cars, gadgets, fashion, household decor – these things are often sold to us on the basis that we need to be seen to be smart, up to date and relevant. It's our desire for respect and a place in our society and community driving this. We are impressed by each other's expressions of material wealth, but the trouble is that you can never keep up. There's always something shinier and newer to want, the absence of which causes fear of being left behind. We would be happier if our social standing wasn't dependent on owning, consuming and displaying. What we really crave is dignity and reasons to feel good about ourselves.

Humans are social mammals. Many of our desires are rooted in how we long to be significant and have social standing. We can't buy meaning. We can't even effectively use objects to get ahead socially, because the whole approach requires us to constantly run after new things while feeling let down by what we have. We're being sold things as substitutes for relationships and community life, but those objects never give what they promise to give and we pay for this financially, emotionally and environmentally.

Chapter 3

Slow Life Sustainability

Life in the slow lane is gentler. Not only does it give us more time to enjoy ourselves, but it costs the planet a good deal less. When we give up the noise and bustle of rushing around, what we get is greater breadth and depth of experience.

The slow living movement has been with us for some time now. Enthusiasts advocate taking the slow options wherever we can and giving up unsatisfying speed and the myth of convenience. When we slow down, we have time to appreciate what's going on. Life in the slow lane offers time to linger over small pleasures, to spend time with people and to invest in quality.

There's no doubt that slowing down is easier if you are well resourced. If your life is dominated by economic pressures, long work hours, insecurity and limited choices, then your scope to be gentle with yourself is limited. For me, the scope to slow down while not being well resourced has had a lot to do with rejecting norms of modern living. Walking is my primary mode of transport. I handwash clothes, I make a lot of things from scratch. It's slower, and cheaper and it takes a lot more of my time and effort, but it also allows me to feel more present in my own life.

With limited resources, you might only be able to choose a few ways to slow down – but it is worth doing so wherever you can. It might mean taking ten minutes outside with a cup of coffee in the morning. It might mean finding an hour in the week for journaling, drawing or some other nourishing practice. Slowing down eases stress and gives us chance to be more on top of our lives. If all you can snatch is minutes here and there, take them and guard them jealously!

Slowing down depends on being able to scrutinise the value

of what we have and what we do. When you're over-stimulated, it can feel impossible to step back and put things in perspective. Stepping away from the phone, the internet and other screens and distractions to just reflect on life, is so valuable. If you're able to do this for an hour or so before bed, there's the bonus that it will help you sleep better. A quiet hour at the end of the day enables reflection and helps us ease towards sleep. If you really can't afford an hour, take what you can manage – ten minutes is worth having if that's what's feasible.

When we start reclaiming time in this way, things change. It becomes possible to see what's using up time to no advantage. I love the internet, but doom scrolling is a terrible activity to get sucked into. So is spending time online arguing with strangers – no matter how good the cause, it gets very little done. However, watching cat videos cheers me greatly, as does talking with friends. I choose to use the internet gently and for my own benefit.

The slow life means cleaning things that are dirty, and only replacing or fixing things that are broken. Replacing things to 'keep up' is a waste of your time and money. It means doing one or two things thoughtfully and enjoyably, not trying to dash through ten 'fun' activities in a morning. It's letting children amuse themselves some of the time, not planning activities for their every waking hour. Boredom is good for children and adults alike, as it invites creativity. If things don't have to be planned, busy, clean, shiny or tidy at all times, we have more opportunity to live.

It's all too easy to use busyness as a distraction. When we're busy little bees, we can persuade ourselves that what we do is virtuous and we can avoid having space for any complicated feelings. We're not going to be happy all the time, some aspects of life will always be miserable and difficult. That's being human for you. It's better to show up for those experiences and to properly feel them rather than trying to drown them out all the time. To be an authentic person, you can't be forever hiding from the feelings you find difficult. We need to make room for grief and fear, loss, regret, frustration, boredom and all the rest. If we aren't consuming to try and avoid our own feelings, we'll consume less.

We're all going to age and die. So much of what we consume involves trying to ignore or deny that truth. If we embrace our mortality and the natural ageing process, we free ourselves from a great deal of pressure. Rather than trying to be what we're not, we can then deploy more resources on actually living and enjoying the time we have. The denial of mortality is the denial of life. Time spent trying to be forever young and immortal is time wasted and life we don't get back.

Slow Fashion

Fast fashion is one of the most destructive industries on the planet. Clothing made to be thrown away wastes a colossal amount of energy and material, and gives us very little in return. Slow fashion, on the other hand, is a long term pleasure.

I really enjoy clothes. I like playing with fabric, and owning new things. I really enjoy having unique items of clothing. I upcycle a lot, I re-work existing garments. I knit. I also salvage fabric from ruined garments and reuse that. The crafting side of this gives me a great deal of entertainment, and I get the pleasure of wearing things that cannot be bought.

If you don't have the skills to do this already, the internet is an amazing resource, full of suggestions and tutorial videos. I learned about boro and sashiko, how to knit jumpers and how to do basic crochet from YouTube videos. Basic skills will get you a long way, and those basic skills are easy to pick up.

Buying vintage and second hand clothing is also a good antidote to fast fashion. All sorts of interesting clothing can be sourced this way. Older garments tend to be better quality and longer lasting than the new items. New is not, in fact better at the moment. New clothing tends to be shoddy, made from poor quality materials and not likely to last.

If you have the budget, buying clothes from makers is also a good choice. It's not cheap, but it does mean you get exactly what you wanted, made perfectly to your size. Most of us aren't well served by the limited clothes sizes available in shops, and this also tends to be an issue when buying second hand. Picking up the skills for being able to alter your own clothes is a really good investment.

Slow Transport

If the cars are backed up in queues, there's a fair chance I will overtake them on foot. As a pedestrian, I have access to all sorts of shortcuts. During peak traffic times, I can get across town faster walking than a person can driving, and I don't have to pay to park at the other end. For the person on a bike, the odds of beating the cars are even greater.

Fast transport isn't actually that fast, especially not in urban environments. The freedom of the open road belongs to people who are not stuck in cars. It's our belief in the speed and utility of cars that keeps us using them, but increasingly what we do in cars is to sit in queues, breathing in the fumes.

If we drove less, urban environments would be much nicer. Cars produce a huge amount of noise and light pollution as well as what they do to the air. Many of us have impaired health as a direct consequence of not being active enough. If we walked and cycled more, we'd be richer, fitter, healthier and we'd live in nicer environments. With fewer cars on the road, buses would have smoother, faster journeys. Those people who really can't walk or cycle would have an easier time finding the parking spaces they need. We'd also need fewer parking spaces – how much of the urban landscape is taken up with places to put cars? How much nicer would our cities be if half of those could be turned into green spaces?

Slow transport gives a great deal. When you're walking, you

have time to mull things over, get mentally ready for where you're going or process what just happened. On foot, you get the chance to greet people. Walking for transport also means getting to see far more wildlife and to encounter the natural world. This is true in the most unlikely places. I spent one weekend at an event on the edge of the Trafford retail park near Manchester – I walked for transport and I saw so many small birds, rabbits, a buzzard and a heron. Nature is far more present than you'd know from a car.

It can be really hard walking in all weathers. However, good quality walking gear is a lot less expensive than car ownership. It is physically demanding to do it day after day – and if you have health problems it really may not be viable. But, there's a lot to be said for taking what you can.

Walking for transport opens up your locality to you. As someone who mostly walks, I notice how car travel distorts a sense of distance and scale. Travelling by car impacts on your relationship with the landscape. You miss all the details. Roads aren't always the quickest ways and traffic systems can really distort your understanding of the geography. Nothing will give you an authentic sense of the landscape like moving your body through it in slower ways.

Slow Food

When you're time poor, pre-prepared food can be a real blessing. Not everyone has the skills or the equipment to cook from scratch. However, as with the sewing, if you want to learn then the internet is full of resources. Being able to cook simple food can save you a lot of money. Cooking doesn't have to be high-end effort laden faff. Basic cooking – like being able to boil vegetables – offers a lot of advantages.

The idea that food has to be massively complicated involving recipes that you follow precisely while using exactly the right equipment, is just another one of those lies designed to part you from your money. Cooking can be fairly quick and simple. It's best to learn theories than recipes – how to make a salad, or a roast dinner, or a stew. Getting the gist of it and then improvising is fun and flexible and allows you to use whatever is cheap or in season.

It can be possible to eat more cheaply if you can do everything from scratch, but it's the getting started that's often most difficult here. Not everyone is going to find this possible. If you don't have the money, building up a decent amount of kitchen equipment is challenging. There's also a lot of bits and pieces – herbs, spices, oil, flours… things that enable cooking that you might struggle to fund on a tight budget.

Ideally, we'd all be buying local food and lovingly cooking it at home in order to have slow sociable meals with our friends and families. Many people are a very long way from living that ideal and just have to do the best they can with what they have. Living in poverty often goes alongside very restricted options for food buying, for cooking, even for owning kitchen equipment.

If your options for slowing down and eating well are limited, here are some suggestions. Take your food breaks away from your work station. Stop to focus on eating if you can, don't do it on the run. Have the nicest things you can afford – poor nutrition does terrible things to health, energy and quality of life. It is more important to have the energy you need than to worry about your weight.

If you can slow down and invest time and care in one meal a day, that's better for you. If you can source some of your food well, that's better for the planet. If you can cut back on some packaging, some waste, then that's all to the good. Tackling food waste is a really good way to reduce your costs and your environmental impact.

Food is emotive. It has a huge environmental impact, and it also has a massive impact on people's health and quality of life. It's really important not to add to this by burdening people with shame when their situations are limited. Do the best you can with what you have.

If you can grow your own – fantastic – but not everyone has a garden or the time and energy to work in one. If you've got access to a farmer's market, wonderful. If you can afford a veg box, that's great too. For the person on a limited budget, being vegetarian can give the best balances of affordability and sustainability.

The diet that does us most good has a large quantity of fresh fruit and vegetables in it. This is the diet that also harms the planet least. There is no conflict between seeking the healthiest diet for yourself and wanting to be sustainable. We also benefit more socially and emotionally from food that we've been able to take time over. Grabbing food on the run isn't good for our bodies, or for our mental health. We enjoy food more when it's interesting, and the bland, mass produced stuff doesn't give us that to any great degree. Food made from scratch tends to involve less packaging, less waste, fewer additives and better nutrition.

Slow Shopping

Shopping is work. It takes time, effort, money and attention. The more pressured we feel to spend time shopping, the less time we have for other things. Knowing what you really want and need saves a great deal of time. Shopping only to replace what needs replacing means we consume far less.

When we are time poor, and obliged to grab in haste whatever will do for now, our shopping is inefficient. The person who can spend more time thinking has to spend less time sourcing things. For example, this year, my vacuum cleaner broke. I had bought it as the easiest thing I could source that would do the job. We took the time to consider as a household what qualities we wanted in a vacuum and to look online at prices and options. The conclusion we came to, was to buy a floor sweeper. It's better than a brush, uses no electricity, is easy to fix if damaged, has few parts, and takes up little space. It will last for years and is low maintenance and costs far less. The time I took to make that decision is time I won't spend emptying vacuum bags – this is far easier to empty out. it's lighter, easier to use, and easier to store. Slowing down leads to making better choices, saving money and creating less waste.

When the aim is to enter a long term relationship with anything you bring home, shopping is more about thought and commitment. Taking the time to figure out exactly what you need results in having exactly what you need. Making do is inefficient, it costs time and money that could be better used elsewhere. The person who knows what they want is less vulnerable to being persuaded into buying something they don't really want or need. Shopping is also far less stressful when you know what you need.

When we shop for prestige and social advantage, shopping is something we have to do a lot of. When we shop for utility, it takes far less time. I like being able to focus entirely on my wants, needs and preferences. I consider myself greatly advantaged by not needing anyone else's approval. Shopping for your social standing costs a lot more emotionally as well as financially. The more at ease you are with yourself, the less you will feel any need to do that.

Slowing Down for Inclusion and Gentleness

High speed living excludes a lot of people. That may be part of the point – speed is an expression of affluence, capability and success. If you are poor, disabled, overworked, ill, depressed... you won't be able to keep up with life in the fast lane. But here's a thing – I'm not attracted to ideas of superiority based on that kind of exclusion. I don't want to be in a fast lane that forces out people who are disadvantaged. I'm much more interested in inclusion and opportunity.

Slow living is more inclusive. It has the time to ask what everyone needs in order to participate, and in the slow lane, you can afford to care about that. If you aren't rushing about trying to prove something, you can care about the people who would otherwise be left behind. In the slow lane, more of us are able to live well.

Aspiring to a slow and gentle life means aspiring not to over consume or to waste things. I reject consumption as an expression of personal power and social significance. I'm just not interested in it. I don't want to compete and I don't want to be seen as competitive. I have no interest in making people feel anything about me based on how much I needlessly consume to try to impress them. There's nothing spiritual in that way of life. There's nothing soulful, meaningful or inherently rewarding.

Chapter 4

Wealth in Relationships

Social connections impact on our identities, sense of self-worth and overall feelings of well-being. We're happiest when we feel valued and respected by the people we, in turn, value and respect. It's a fundamental human urge and one that is easily diverted towards consumption.

If we seek our wealth in relationships rather than in possessions, we have the scope to do ourselves considerable good. Impressing people with our actions is far easier than trying to buy kudos – for a start there isn't the pressure to keep up. Your reputation and how you are seen by people around you is something you can build and sustain in much gentler ways.

There are many ways a person can shine. We might do it through excellence – in work, in creativity, in sports, fundraising, running community events. We might do it through kindness – in our small daily interactions or manifesting that as bigger gestures. Generosity is an easy quality to cultivate and those of us who don't have money can give of our time, care and attention or share other resources. Knowledge and wisdom are valuable things to offer to those around you. Humour is often greatly appreciated by other humans.

The bar can be quite low set on this. You don't have to be an extraordinary person to be appreciated by those around you. Online, people who simply share small beauties are often really popular with their friends. Putting everyday nice things in front of people provides comfort and cheer, which has considerable value.

We can be praise-givers. This is actually a really strong social position to take. If you make it your job to praise, appreciate, lift and encourage the people around you, then you'll help them, and be socially valued yourself. Everyone likes positive feedback. While it's more fashionable to criticise, in my experience people learn and improve tremendously when you simply point out to them the things they do that work, or are particularly good. We grow when we are nourished by encouragement. Giving praise and watching a person develop thanks to that is a fantastic way to live and to engage with other people.

Getting to shine socially isn't a competitive activity. You don't have to be better than anyone else for it to work. We can all lift each other. And how wonderful it is to be surrounded by people who are brilliant, kind, interesting, generous, inventive and so forth. Seeing the best qualities in those around you and honouring that is a way of giving to other people. It enriches your social experience, and in seeking the good, it also gives you more to enjoy.

When we set out to appreciate each other and build each other up, wonderful things happen. Most people rise to the opportunity when given a chance to be their best selves. We all do a better job when we've got an appreciative audience – whether that's a question of how we do our parenting, how we do our hair, or what we want to talk about. An appreciative audience makes a person want to be their best self. The more time you spend trying to be your best self, the more you get to feel that's who you are, and the more you become that person.

As I said before, your most authentic self is who you choose to be. When we do that collectively, setting out to bring out the best in each other, we all grow together. At the same time, we grow in confidence, we feel more able and more powerful and we start doing the things we really want to do.

Spiritual Community

One of the major attractions of the spiritual life is participation in community. Being part of a spiritual community can contribute significantly to a person's sense of self. Feeling recognised and respected within a spiritual community can provide a healthy antidote to consumerism, protecting us from having our basic needs exploited.

In theory, the world's religions encourage us to avoid greed and over consumption. Of course, in practice it isn't always that simple. There is a relationship between spirituality and consumerism, and it can be the problem rather than the solution.

For Pagans, there are plenty of suppliers keen to help us look the part. Clothes and home decor are the principle manifestations of a Pagan aesthetic, but there's also a significant market for tools, crystals, ingredients, spell materials and so forth. Buying your Paganism can be really expensive. Having objects that reinforce our sense of identity is, of course, affirming and empowering. Filling your home with crystals or green men doesn't actually make you a Pagan, but it will help you feel more Pagan. It is the desire to feel certain ways that makes us most vulnerable to commercial exploitation.

There are always people selling shortcuts – whether that's the secret to fixing your life in five minutes, becoming a shaman in a weekend or learning everything you need to know about witchcraft in a week. Short cuts are always tempting for people who feel time poor. They're also meaningless for the genuine seeker. It's not about achieving an end; the point of the path is to travel the path.

New Age commercialism is a considerable problem. This often includes appropriation of indigenous practises and tools, overpriced courses, gratuitous displays of privilege, unsustainable travel to do 'spiritual' things in exotic locations and increasingly fascist elements creeping in. The spirituality you mostly buy isn't actually spiritual, it's just a form of manipulative consumerism, no more sustainable or spiritual than any other act of excessive consumption.

In the Pagan community we also suffer from issues around not being willing to pay people what they are worth, or what their work is worth. Capitalism exploits resources and people alike and has taught us to expect low prices. We should be supporting our creators, and recognising that a hand carved statue has a different value from a mass produced thing that came out of a mould, for example. A consultation with an experienced practitioner is worth a lot more than a badly made spell kit that might actually set your house on fire.

It's important to think about how and why we spend money in relation to our spiritual practises. What, exactly, are we buying, and from whom? Who do we benefit with what we buy, and who pays a cost for it? As in all things, if we seek durable, meaningful acquisitions that we intend to have long term relationships with, that's probably not going to cause problems. If we're buying someone else's sacred plant where that plant is at risk of extinction because of commercial demand... we're not being spiritual.

There is justice inherent in paying fairly. There is nothing un-spiritual about trading with each other for knowledge, resources, unique creations and so forth. Money itself is not a problem and fair exchange is honourable and appropriate. What we need to watch out for is exploitation and those situations where we are invited to spend money just to feel a certain way about ourselves without doing the work.

Seeking Kudos

The desire for kudos is easily co-opted. Rather than earning it through our actions, we try to acquire it through brand choices, makes of car, fashion statements and the like. To a certain degree this works – as long as the people around us are persuaded to value the same things, and we can keep affording the upgrades all the time.

It's much more sustainable to seek kudos based on personal qualities and actions, rather than on spending power. When your sense of self depends on spending, it's easy to end up spiralling into debt just trying to keep up appearances. Setbacks loom large if they also mean you could lose your social standing. If your identity depends on your disposable income, then you are incredibly vulnerable.

The standard self-esteem advice is not to base your sense of worth on achievements. However, this is far better for you than basing it on your economic power. When your sense of self depends on who you are and what you can do – you have a decent chance of maintaining that no matter what happens. Your knowledge, skills, experience and personal virtues remain yours no matter what. No one can take those things from you, or price you out of them. Even if you lose something of that to accident or illness, it was still yours. You are not one pay check away from losing your imagination, compassion or humour, even though you could easily be one pay check from losing your material wealth.

It should be obvious that seeking kudos through competitive spending can't work. We have finite resources and we're pushing the planet to the brink. If we keep on like this, all we will have left to fight over is who can sit on the biggest landfill heap. Competitive acquisition is totally unsustainable and there's not much joy in it. However, there are better ways to seek kudos.

We just need to ditch the idea that innate talent is important, and scarce. I see this a lot around my creative work – that many believe talent is the important thing, and that they have none and therefore can't do anything. In my experience, raw talent is of little consequence – enthusiasm is more important. Passion for something so that you invest in it is what makes the real difference, and ten thousand hours of work will make you a highly skilled expert at pretty much anything.

If you are willing to put in the time, you can be good at anything. This doesn't mean you'll be able to do it for money – there's a lot of luck and privilege tied up in that. There are some things it's hard to get into without money and opportunities, and too many things that exclude people based on disability, race and gender. But even so, the basic principle stands – you are more than a consumer, you can do more than consume. There are much greater emotional and practical rewards available for learning and using skills. There's also joy to be had in the learning process, in seeing yourself improve and in connecting with people who share your enthusiasm.

Community Action

Taking part in community action answers the emotional need for recognition and involvement while tackling problems head on. Dealing with the climate emergency alone is daunting and can be harrowing. When we unite with others, not only do we get more done, but we increase our emotional resilience. It's easier to face these things together. Successful community action helps reduce the fear and the despair we might otherwise experience.

Community action takes many forms, and you can pick a way of getting involved that plays to your strengths and interests. You may choose a political route, focusing on change from above, petitions, campaigns, protests and the like. You could join a party, stand for election, raise issues that are key to you. Or you might prefer to do the same sort of work through a charity or an organisation.

It may make more sense to you to focus on making physical changes – you might get involved with a local tree planting group, help care for the land in some way or fundraise for environmental regeneration. Your community action might involve a local gardening project, or your local park. There are many environmental organisations that need volunteers in all kinds of capacities.

You can focus on social justice, on feeding the poor and sheltering the homeless. There are many organisations involved with raising the quality of life for the disadvantaged. This may not seem relevant in the climate fight, but it is. There is a profound connection between inequality and environmental damage. The projects that challenge the idea that wealth accumulation is good and that a person's worth is economic, are always worth getting involved with.

Building community is itself a way of improving resilience. When people get together, the scope for direct action increases. People who meet up and talk are going to be more open to doing things as a community, and from that sense of community all kinds of changes can occur. Creating or supporting community spaces is itself a really valuable action to take.

You might have a specific skill you can bring to bear. My local Transition town groups include a repair cafe, a group focused on keeping fabric out of landfill, a group working to reduce plastic waste and a group that grows edible plants in public places. All kinds of different skills are called for here! I was able to use my writing and social media skills to help promote what was going on for this group, and for other local concerns. Whatever you can do, there will be a way to make good use of it.

If you can't do the physical activism, there's a lot of good work to be done online. Often this can be done when it suits you. I've spent years quietly raising awareness of the value of trees and woodland – especially ancient woodland – as part of my volunteering work for The Woodland Trust.

There's a lot a person can do alone with solitary actions, but so much more that we can do when we work together. There's a real joy to be found in working with other people to get something meaningful done – often our normal jobs don't give us that feeling of satisfaction and significance. When we feel that what we do has meaning, we feel better about ourselves and don't need to comfort ourselves by purchasing things.

Privilege and Prejudice

Building community doesn't just mean encountering people very much like ourselves. Resilient communities are bigger than that and embrace more people. Animist communities can also recognise and embrace people who are not humans. To make this work, it really helps if we all spend a bit of time looking at our own privileges and prejudices.

Privilege is often hard to spot. It's the things we have that others don't, that we don't automatically see. Wealthy people often ascribe their wealth to effort, not to luck even though the most reliable predictor for wealth remains having wealthy parents. Privilege often involves the things we take for granted – education, an able body, being neurotypical and so forth. If you think of yourself as 'normal' give some serious thought to what you consider 'abnormal' and how that may impact on your treatment of people who are different from you.

Prejudice and privilege are often closely related. Privilege is easily explained and justified by what we imagine about 'those other people'. Who do you consider to be inferior to you? Why might their situation be different to yours? If you don't know much about that group of people, try to learn more. Education helps us overcome fear, develop compassion and empathy, and better relate to each other. For example, knowing that substance abuse is often linked to trauma is likely to change how a person feels about addiction. When you understand why battered women don't always leave violent men, you may feel very differently about those situations.

The New Age movement is terrible for reinforcing prejudice. It adds in layers about spiritual worthiness, willingness to manifest change, pre-life agreements and suchlike. When we imagine that we do not suffer because we are superior, we miss the many roles that fortune and opportunity play in our lives. It's very hard to make good choices when you don't have any good options in front of you. It's easier to make dramatic changes and remarkable leaps of faith when you have plenty of money.

This doesn't mean letting people off the hook for bad choices. It doesn't mean giving anyone a free pass, or allowing ourselves not to take any responsibility for dealing with things we have limited control over. We all have to try and make the best we can of what we have. When we can see the kinds of challenges other people face, we can learn to meet that with compassion and at the very least not to make things worse.

The Power of Sharing

Sharing makes bonds within communities. It is a means by which we can lift and help each other. This can be about the sharing of resources or money, but often this isn't the most important thing. The most precious thing a human can choose to share, is their time. When we offer our time to each other, we are stepping away from economic relationships and towards something much more authentic.

We can share skills, stories, ideas, dreams, hopes and fears. Talking about our lives, and especially our inner lives is a really powerful kind of sharing. So let me tell you about some of the things that happened to me today.

Two friends gave me their dead jeans. I've salvaged pockets and waistband material. I'm now making that into a waist belt of pockets for another friend, who hopefully will be cheered by this. Meanwhile, a friend who lives further away posted me some lovely handmade gloves and a friend in another country showed me photos from the train trip he is on. I'm writing this section because the friend who test-read the first draft of the book felt there weren't enough stories in this bit of it. These are all stories about gifting, and the sharing of stories is really important in building relationships, communities and new ways of being in the world.

When you feel like an authentic person dealing with authentic people, it's much easier to show up. Sharing thoughts and feelings when we know that will be welcome isn't exposed or scary. When we share stories that reflect our inner lives, we deepen bonds and develop greater understanding of each other.

This way lies emotional security and feelings of belonging and involvement. You just can't buy that, and trying to buy it makes us worse off.

Patriarchal capitalism has us focused into nuclear families. We are supposed to live with one other adult who is everything to us. The stories we tell each other about relationships are narrow and inhibiting. Sharing yourself with more people makes you, and them, more resilient. Exploring love outside of romance, and outside of sexual relationships and family bonds is a really good idea. There are so many ways of relating to each other and connecting with each other, and that all begins with sharing our time, and sharing something of ourselves.

Chapter 5

Creativity for All

When reading Rob Hopkins' excellent book, *From What Is to What If*, I was struck by his observations about imagination. If we can't imagine a better world, we're going to have a hard time creating one. Being able to imagine is an essential skill for moving towards more sustainable ways of life. It's also critically important for our quality of life and our wellbeing.

Imagination is key to all problem solving and all creativity. To find a solution, we have to look at what we've got and see how it could be different. Logic and rational thinking will help us examine what's in front of us, but it takes imagination to make a leap from there into seeing the scope for change. If all we can contemplate is life as we currently experience it, change is unthinkable and threatening. If we can imagine change as bringing us good things, it's a lot more persuasive than if we take onboard the idea that we're being told to go back to the Stone Age. I've seen the right wing media presenting sustainability in precisely these terms and it's neither encouraging, nor fair representation of said Stone Age!

Every part of our lives can be enriched by our own imaginative thinking and ability to be creative. When we do more for ourselves, it's empowering, expressive, rewarding and interesting. There is happiness to be found in having ideas and being able to implement them. Everyone should be entitled to the time and resources for creative expression, imaginative exploration and having fun with making things.

Imagination requires time. You need peaceful hours when you aren't on call or over-stimulated. You need to be rested, to have had chance to process your thoughts and feelings, and to feel free from pressures or the need to be doing something else.

Imagination depends on having some space to let your mind wander and make connections between things.

In many ways, imagination is like a muscle and if it isn't used, it gets weak. It takes time and practice to get your imagination into shape, able to lift loads, run wildly into the future, dismantle systems and build possibilities. We do better with this when we're supported by opportunities, and by each other. Shared space for creativity is a great way of building imaginative muscle.

Everyone should have access to the arts for the sheer joy of it. Dance, performance, theatre, making images and objects, telling stories, encountering poems. It's good to do this as an audience, and it's also important to step into some of that as an active participant and creator. Art should not be for some special few – and when it is elitist, that isn't because the people allowed to do it are better creators. The creative industries are not meritocracies. The people who succeed aren't more deserving of success than everyone else and almost always it's because they have more money and privilege than most of us. Art must be for everyone.

When we have space to explore creativity in whatever forms we like, we can become imaginative and creative people. Obvious art forms can be a good way of getting your mind warmed up to creative thinking, but any aspect of life can be handled creatively. Any problem we face requires a creative solution. Anything we want to improve, we need to be able to dream about. For most of human history, we've made our solutions – as individuals, as households, as communities. We've dreamed together and we've made the answers, often with our own hands. Mass production robs us of this. Convenience shopping encourages us not to find or create our own ways of being and doing. We save time, but for what? We deny ourselves expression and all kinds of emotional rewards.

Better Ways are Possible

We can stop dreaming about wealth, property and competing

with others. We can stop assuming that what we have now is inevitable and unchangeable. We can reject the stories that tell us constant growth is the only route to better things and that progress is measured in material wealth for the few. Anything can be changed. To live sustainably, we're going to have to change our shared stories, our lives, and how we see ourselves. We won't do that if we think it means giving up on all the 'good stuff'.

Sitting in traffic while commuting isn't good stuff. Being in debt isn't good stuff. Being hungry, stressed and lonely most certainly isn't anything to aspire to. Apparently, we spend more time working now than your typical mediaeval peasant did. We're not happy, we have an epidemic of mental illness much of which can be ascribed to stress, poverty, work and loneliness. We have the resources to take care of everyone and yet we don't. The wealth gap grows, and the planet is dying. Capitalism doesn't work for most of us.

Better ways are possible – it is down to us to imagine other ways of living. We have everything we need to do that. Every single one of us is capable of imagining something better. Many of us are capable of acting on those ideas. When we do, we need to make a point of including the people most limited by poverty and disability so that they are lifted into greater opportunities too. The sustainable revolution has to be inclusive.

It has never been more important to think about what you want from life. Do you want clean air and safe drinking water? Do you want food that will make you well, or are you happy to eat things that undermine your health and have huge environmental costs? How much of your life do you want to spend sat in a car that isn't moving? How much of your surroundings do you enjoy seeing covered with tarmac? Are you willing to accept obscene inequality so that the rich can have ever more? Or do you want to live in a fair and just society that actually has a future? Do you want the time and resources to actually enjoy your life rather than just trying to survive and bear it as best you can?

We've been lied to, relentlessly about what makes for a good life and how to achieve that. Progress based on unchecked growth is a lie that is going to kill us. Trickle-down economics is a lie. The idea that the super-rich are good for us, is a lie. The idea that hard work will lift you out of poverty, is a lie. If we accept that fairness, justice and equality are unrealistic, then they will remain so. If we set out to change ourselves and our cultures so that we live fairly and sustainably, we can do that. Cultures are just people. If enough people set out to make change, then the culture changes. If we stop idolising wealth and treating obscene overconsumption as glamorous and attractive, things will change. If we support each other rather than shaming those who are in need, things will change. Better things are possible if enough of us assert that it is so.

Following the Bard Path

The bard path is very much part of modern Druidry and there's every reason to think it was an important spiritual and social role for our ancestors as well. Historical bards focused on music, poetry, story and history. For the modern bard, other forms of creativity are also considered valid.

When I made my dedication to the bard path, I promised – as many other modern bards do – to use my creativity for the good of my people, and for the good of the land. I live that promise from day to day in all kinds of ways.

I use my creativity to upcycle and reuse fabric. I share what I'm doing with the intention of inspiring others to have a go. I use my writing skills to speak for woodland and to encourage people to care about trees. Each February, I use my creative skills to support the Show The Love campaign, raising awareness of climate change impact. I use poetry particularly to try and inspire people with feelings of care and engagement about the land. I use my fiction writing to explore philosophical issues and to express ideas about how humans interact.

It doesn't work to be too preachy. Books like this only engage people like you, dear reader, who already want to move towards this work. However, most people don't respond well to being lectured. Part of the work of the modern bard is to inspire and uplift people so that they feel able to act. Through creativity we can build community and seed ideas for change. We can lead by example, showing more creative approaches to modern life, and how much fun that can be. When we share beauty and inspiration, we enrich the people who encounter it. Fighting against things is emotionally exhausting. As bards we can remind people that they can also stand up for love, for beauty and peace, for richer and more meaningful lives, for happiness, health and hope.

People aren't reliably moved by facts or science. It doesn't help that the facts we face are so brutal and impact on a scale it is difficult for many of us to even think about. Humans do, however, respond to songs and stories – these things have been with us for as long as we've been humans, if not longer. Stories have the power to make large scale things personal, relatable and coherent. As bards we can work to take the painful truths, overwhelming problems and cold facts, and turn them into something personal and possible to think about. Alongside this, we need stories that map the way to better futures and that offer hope.

We need to tell each other that we can do great things through cooperation, and that fair sharing is so much better than competition. We need stories about how we might flourish together, and stories in which violence is not the answer. Many such stories do already exist, but we need more. This isn't just about published fiction, either. We tell each other stories every day – drawn from experience, and from whatever culture we're absorbing. We can be deliberate about the kinds of stories we share. We can avoid the jokes that punch down or that reinforce stereotypes and prejudice. With the news so full of misery, we can do a lot of good simply by sharing the more encouraging stories with each other. When everything seems terrible, the futility can be overwhelming. Good stories about real change will help offset this.

If you are already out in the world as a creative person, one of the most powerful things you can do is to help other people create as well. Creating empowers people and opens the way to making change. When we can create, we can be more independent, and at the same time we can interact with each other based on exchanges that are dignified and meaningful. When people can express themselves creatively, and make practical solutions, they are standing in their own power and less vulnerable to manipulation. Creativity fosters self-respect, and people who have good reason to think well of themselves are better placed to be inclusive, compassionate and cooperative. Many of our social ills stem from people trying to boost their own self-esteem by knocking someone else down.

People grow when they are given space to do so. Skills are developed simply by spending time doing things. If it is fine to make mistakes, and fine not to be great when you start out, there is room to learn and experiment. It's important not to hold learners to professional standards. Critical feedback isn't of much use to most people and is more likely to knock them back than advance them. Support and encouragement gets a lot more done.

Nourished by our own Creativity

The act of creating is itself nourishing in all kinds of ways. When we engage with artistic forms and with more practical kinds of creativity, we find out things about ourselves. In expressing ourselves creatively, we also explore our own identities, values and feelings. This can be just as true for someone working in a kitchen or garden as it is for someone working at an easel or a piano. Finding out what you want to engage with is itself a precious door into your own most authentic self.

Some people create in a frenzy of inspiration. Mostly that's not how it works though, and for most of us, creativity is a balance of research, study, planning, discipline and those wilder, more unpredictable things that come from having a free-range mind. Inspiration can be applied to all aspects of life, but it's more likely to show up if we deliberately seek it and make time for it.

Some people use journaling for self-knowledge, but it doesn't work for everyone. That creative exploration of self, and self-in-context can be undertaken just as well by maintaining an altar, working in a garden, planting a wood, or learning a song. These actions are all full of choices that will reveal us to ourselves if we're paying attention. At the same time, anything you do can be approached thoughtfully and undertaken as an art form. Anything can be undertaken with an eye to grace, beauty, virtue and value.

When we make more time for beauty, our lives are enriched. Finding out what seems beautiful to you is a process of self-exploration. It's another opportunity to throw off the dreams you've been sold in favour of finding the things that really stir your soul. I find beauty in the clutter of a life richly lived, in a home strewn with books, craft projects in progress, houseplants, cats, and cheerful chaos. Others will find soulfulness and peace in minimalism and that's fine – we're all different and every response is valid.

We gain more nourishment from things we interact with than we do from passive consumption or convenience shopping. The things we invest in give back much more than the things we just own. Occasional purchases made with care give us far more than grabbing a mass of unconsidered things in the hopes of feeling something. When we seek beauty in our lives, we start to consider what it is that we love – or could love – and we pour ourselves into what we do and what we own. The trick is not to get derailed by competitiveness. A love of houseplants will greatly enrich your home and life. A desire to have the kind of houseplant photos that get you social media attention may drive you into debt, cause you stress and have you chasing rewards that depend on consumption and display.

When we seek to nourish ourselves primarily through our own actions, we start to pull free of what consumer culture does to us. This becomes even more affecting when we are able to share nourishment with others. The exchange of creativity, and of things we have poured love into opens up a wealth of possibility. I am deeply blessed in this regard in that I interact regularly with other people whose creativity I admire. My own making and imagining is fertilised by seeing what my friends are doing. I am more able to create as a consequence. Further, knowing that my creations uplift and encourage others, I feel secure in my social standing and engaged with other people in a meaningful way.

By conventional standards, I am a shabby goblin. I have no possessions that I can show off to demonstrate wealth – I own a lot of old, worn, second hand, long used things. But my friends are people who are much the same as me. We take pride in our re-purposing skills, our mending skills and our ability to innovate. Consumer culture is just a form of culture, and simply something a lot of people have agreed to go along with. Other cultures are possible, and a good deal more fun to be part of.

Chapter 6

Privilege, Poverty, Inclusion

Sustainability cannot be just a middle class hobby. It has to include everyone. As things stand, it is evidently the case that those with the most wealth cause most damage. For people living in poverty, the odds are that they will have much lower carbon footprints. However, there are a lot of things you can't do if you are poor.

Better insulation saves money and carbon alike. Renewable energy is cheaper once you have it installed. Organic food is pricey, and it can be impossible to source locally grown food without a car. If you don't have money, the odds are you won't have a garden and can't grow your own. Low impact living depends on having resources and space – if your home is overcrowded and you don't have a decent kitchen, avoiding single use plastic is a lot harder. People living hand to mouth cannot afford sustainable options and end up spending far more on repeatedly buying low quality things that fall apart easily and have to be thrown away.

Economically speaking, the redistribution of wealth is an essential component of greener living. We cannot afford people being in such abject poverty that they cut down their trees for short term survival. Intense poverty harms landscapes around the world, and most often those problems are caused by wealthier nations creating debt, demanding unsustainable cash crops, causing war and refusing to pay fairly for goods.

The single most useful thing you can do on your own in the face of this, is to stop shaming and blaming poor people for circumstances they have no control over. The belief that poor people are the problem fuels eco-fascism and encourages the acceptance of the death and suffering of the poorest and most vulnerable people on the planet. This is hideous. It also solves nothing for any of us and diverts attention from the real problems.

Any local projects you are involved with need to be inclusive. It's not enough to have high cost interventions where middle class people get to feel smug even though they're still buying massive cars and flying off regularly for holidays. If sustainable living looks smug and hypocritical, it will encourage resentment, not participation. The intention of lifting the disadvantaged needs hard-wiring into every sustainability action. Organic hummus does not offset long haul flights. It may be really uncomfortable for those who have a great deal to have to recognise that and actually cut back on ownership and consumption, but this is necessary. Blaming poor people is easy, and changes nothing for the good. Those who have most have work to do recognising the need for fairer sharing, and acting on that by taking less.

The world's billionaires obviously need to step up to these issues. In the meantime we can help them be more socially responsible by demanding they pay fair tax, protesting their destructive behaviour and avoiding giving them money. Who are we buying from when we take more than we need?

Spirituality and Privilege

There's a lot of privilege tied up in many ideas that claim to be spiritual. Money attracts money, and that's the only like-attracts-like truth of any great consequence. If we overlook the way in which money facilitates so many aspects of capitalist life, we can mistake our good fortune for spiritual advancement. It's easier to manifest your dreams when you can also afford to bankroll them. It's easier to take wild leaps of intuition if you have a financial safety net. Money might not solve everything, but there's a lot it can ease, enable and smooth over.

Life without privilege is often a life with few options. Hard work won't reliably lift you out of poverty. It's easy to make good choices when you have lots of opportunities open to you, and also easy not to notice how blessed you were to begin with.

If we let ourselves mistake privilege for spirituality, we can end up treating badly the people who are most disadvantaged. I see too much of this in New Age thinking. All kinds of toxic positivity exists, blaming people who aren't positive enough to miraculously cure their ailments, overcome their traumas or escape from deprivation. Any notion that involves blaming or shaming people should be considered suspect. All we get from such approaches is more misery for those already in trouble, and superiority complexes for those who have so far been lucky.

This way lies delusion and cognitive dissonance. If we have to believe that every terrible thing we experience happened because we wrote it into our pre-life contract this will likely make us less able to cope, not more so. If we insist on being positive all the time, we don't deal with our grief and anger, our fear or distress. Our so-called negative human emotions are just as real and authentic as the more comfortable ones. They can be great teachers. At the same time, we're not obliged to draw deep meaning from every shitty experience we have. Sometimes the only lesson is that we've just been through something awful.

To be authentic, we have to be realistic. We have to be able to see what comes to us from privilege and not ascribe that to our magical manifesting powers. We need compassion – for ourselves and for others and it's hard to have one without the other. When we have no compassion for others, the compassion we have for ourselves is likely to be fragile and shattered by any fall from wealth or status.

Seeking authenticity demands that we don't make up outrageous stories about why we are better and more deserving than other people. If we imagine our spiritual identities justify our taking more than others have, we're in trouble. If we believe that we're worth more than other people, we're going places that are at odds with spiritual life.

In theory, our spiritual paths should teach us compassion

and humility. Whether you feel we are all one, or all possessed of a divine spark, all part of the web of life, all connected by the Force, or the Tao or anything else... religions and spirituality teach connection and interconnectedness. We're here to ease each other's suffering, to light the way for each other, to lift the downtrodden. Anything designed to comfort the comfortable and distress the uncomfortable is highly suspect and should be avoided.

Inclusion as Transformation

Inclusion is itself radical. Capitalist cultures encourage us to see people in purely economic terms, and it's so ingrained that all too often we don't see the mechanics involved. If you are disadvantaged – be that by race, disability sexual identity, mental illness, neurodiversity, learning difficulties, impoverished background, abuse, fleeing violence – you are likely to be less economically active or successful. Capitalist culture is not set up to include you because the whole thing revolves around economic activity.

Almost any excluding disadvantage you can think of also increases a person's chances of being poor. Difference is discouraged, and all too often excluded from employment opportunities in systems where employed work is the only real option. Those unable to work face abject poverty and social humiliation. This isn't an accident; it is an inevitable consequence of valuing people based on their earning power. Poverty causes exclusion and denies people opportunities. We then reinforce ideas of worthlessness by shaming, blaming and further excluding the people deemed not to be worth enough money.

Including people is a good way of pushing back. Make the space. Look to see who isn't in the room and ask what it might take for them to be there. Don't accept all white, all male, all middle-class membership as either inevitable or appropriate. It can be challenging for people with privilege to notice who isn't in the room. It takes effort to learn about barriers and even more effort to make changes that remove barriers. We have to start by imagining that the absent people matter.

Inclusion can mean meeting somewhere with accessible toilets. It can mean being somewhere people can get to on public transport. The cost of attending, the dress code, and the menu can all serve to exclude people. How do we include people suffering from mental illness? How do we make an activity available to a single parent, or to someone suffering from chronic fatigue? What resources are there that could be deployed? What's wanted, what's needed? We have to be willing to listen, to care and to take action.

Participation in life and society should not be based on ability to pay. Experiencing disadvantages should not leave people in such poverty that they cannot participate in community life – but all too often that's exactly what happens. Anything we can do to improve access and include more people is a pushback against the idea that a person is defined by their pay check. We urgently need to stop seeing people as economic units and start seeing them as living, feeling beings. While we struggle to feel compassion for our own species, we're also going to have a hard time caring about other species, or landscapes.

We are poorer as people when we only encounter people who are just like us. Our understanding of life and humanity is narrowed when we live in narrow communities. For most of history, most humans have lived in extended families and communities – not just with one opposite sex partner. We didn't used to only socialise with people of a similar age to us. We're more divided by income than ever as pay gaps widen. How do we discover richness and diversity within ourselves if there is no variety in our lives?

Our authentic selves might not fit so well in those exclusively white, male, able bodied, middle class spaces. We might feel more pressured to conform when we don't tick all the boxes, rather than demanding that spaces stretch and soften to accommodate us. It's difficult, and I know this from experience, being the one person in the room who does not fit neatly in. The one person who can't afford what everyone else is talking about. The one person who does not conform to everyone else's heteronormativeness... How hard is it to be the only black woman in a room full of white men? The only person speaking English as a second language? The only person participating while in overwhelming physical pain? How difficult is it to participate when your very existence defies the norms of a group?

Active inclusion means caring enough to listen. It can be uncomfortable, facing up to the cultural features you participate in that exclude other people. It means accepting that being white, male, middle class and able bodied is not the benchmark for normal, nor does it equate to being entitled to lead everything and decide how everything will work. Inclusion means those who have most power being willing to use it to give more power to others. There's a history of violence, prejudice, domination and abuse underpinning all of these dynamics, and it takes a certain amount of courage to face that, and refuse to keep participating in it.

Lift and Empower Each Other

There are so many ways to do this. When we are confident in ourselves, we don't need other people to be less powerful. Authenticity gifts us with freedom from the need to dominate and control others. Only fearful, insecure and dysfunctional people are comforted by having power over other people. When we feel authentic and empowered, we don't need to crush anyone else or try to stop them from participating. If you are standing in your own power, you have no reason to be afraid just because someone else is doing the same thing.

If someone asks for help, take them seriously. If changes need to be made to include more people, look at how to do that. If people with privilege are inclined to ignore people who need help participating, be ready to challenge over that. Don't sit in silence when faced with racism or sexism or anything else of that ilk. Call it out at the time. Don't do it in a private way that protects the offender from having their feelings hurt! Make sure the people who urgently need support know that you are supporting them. Don't ask the people who have least to adapt so as to make life easier for those who have most. Don't allow tone policing when someone is upset – that they are upset should be the most important thing. This is by no means an exhaustive list, but it's a place to start. Inclusion has to be active and sometimes means making comfortable people a little uncomfortable.

Kindness isn't weakness at all. Kindness comes from places of strength and self-knowledge. Compassion is a consequence of being free from the kinds of weakness that lead us to hate, fear and resent other people. If no one can make us feel small then we don't have to be afraid. Instead of being mired in jealousy, anxiety and bitterness, we can simply work together to create better ways of living. Authenticity is how we become able to have power-with other people, rather than being trapped in the limiting and fearful states of wanting power-over people.

No amount of authenticity will protect you from people who hold power over you and abuse that power. Sometimes, as with domestic violence, the only way out of that is to leave. When it comes to systemic violence, the solutions will often require other people stepping up – to end workplace bullying, to end prejudicial politics, to dismantle old and abusive approaches.

When we lift and support other people, we are also working to release our competitive, anxious feelings and to throw off the burden of any jealousy we might be carrying. In supporting other people we also help ourselves to feel strong, capable, generous and so forth. These are all virtues to feel good about, and that enhance a person's sense of being intrinsically worthwhile. When we support each other, we all become stronger, more resilient and better resourced.

There are all kinds of ways in which we can do this. Whether it's formally organised, or informal, we can share resources. This might mean tools, knowledge, skills, time, labour, car sharing, or any other form of mutual aid. We can come together in unions, cooperatives, social enterprises, charities, campaigning groups, and more. We can help each other participate by holding doors open, removing glass ceilings, and being alert to the risk of accidentally excluding others. We can better resource each other by giving away what we no longer need. We can normalise asking for help and make a point of treating people with both kindness and respect if they express need. If we treat it as a privilege to be able to help, we can do so without being condescending. It is vital to help people in the ways that they find helpful, and not go round imposing values and assumptions on other people. When we listen and care, we will find more to respect in ourselves and in other people.

Beyond Economic Measures

When we make an effort to include people, we stop treating them as economic units. We urgently need to let go of the idea that a person's value is tied to their economic worth. It's a belief that distorts human relationships and that skews our societies. The things that pay most are not the things most essential to the functioning of our societies. The things that most improve our comfort and mental health are also not things that pay well. The greatest wealth tends to be accumulated by people who are able to make money out of money – a process that depletes others, and the environment, and gives nothing in return.

If we valued life for its own sake, we'd have to rethink everything. Our societies would be obliged to stop treating the ill, and the poor as disposable and insignificant. We would also have to change our relationship with the natural world. Given how human-centric humans tend to be, we will probably need to change our relationships with each other before we can adopt the wider idea of valuing life more than we value money.

At the moment, we treat nature based on its economic worth. We're interested in what can be bought and sold. We depend on nature to deal with our waste and mess, but we don't even budget that in properly to our shoddy economic thinking. We don't measure the economic value of the mental health benefits trees give us, or the general health benefits we might get from clean air and safe water. We don't look at what climate chaos is likely to cost and factor that in, but instead our governments whimper over the expense of trying to avoid all of that. As though carrying on as we are until we're extinct makes good economic sense.

What is a tree worth? What happens when we see it not as potential timber, or paper, but as a living, breathing entity? What happens when we treat living creatures with respect and assume that we are not automatically entitled to exploit them in any way we please? That might not disincline us to eat them, but it would have to mean raising them with care, protecting their environments, and never considering it acceptable to slaughter them only to send their bodies to landfill.

What happens when we see our landscapes as genuine presences worthy of our care and respect? How much would change if the value of land wasn't measured in the resources we can extract from it or the profits to be made 'developing' and selling it. What if we stopped describing building as developing? We talk about human impacts on the land as though they are inherently improving – because all we see is that we've improved the economic value of a place. But we may well have destroyed its ecosystem. We need to understand these things differently.

Chapter 7

Political Changes

While I'm primarily interested in personal and grass roots changes, we can't do everything that way. There are some things that would make a huge difference that really need political engagement. However, to get political engagement we need to build awareness and get people involved with the ideas. In each case, these are changes that would improve quality of life for people.

The barrier to these changes is always money. It may be the idea that we just can't afford to do this – which is simply untrue. Money is just a system for moving things around, and new money is mostly imagined into existence by banks providing loans for mortgages. We can do anything we like with money, none of these things are impossible and plenty of non-traditional economists talk about them.

These changes would, of course, impact on people who benefit from exploiting others. They have all kinds of stories to justify doing things their way and will insist that everything would fall apart without them. But they take far more than they give and it would not be prohibitively difficult to reorganise things on better terms.

The other arguments against such changes tend to revolve around the idea that work is morally good for people. Without the threat of abject poverty, most people would be too lazy to work – we're encouraged to believe. When you consider how many people give their time to unpaid work, it really doesn't bear scrutiny. This is the logic of the Victorian workhouse. The majority of people are motivated by the desire for community standing and purposeful living, and will engage on those terms. Living in fear of abject poverty should not be seen as good or desirable. Drudgery and exploitation does not ennoble or enable anyone. It's also worth considering that if all work was genuinely good for you, the upper classes would be a lot keener on doing it themselves.

Right to Repair

Built in obsolescence fuels consumerism, is expensive for us and terrible for the planet. However, without laws giving us the right to repair, and requiring companies to make repairable items and keep parts in stock, we won't have that. Repair cafes are great, but there are limits to what they can do.

Being able to repair things is empowering, dignified and saves money as well as reducing our impact on the planet. Having items for longer means we can have more meaningful relationships with them. The economic models that depend on us throwing things away and getting new ones are utterly unsustainable and unsuitable for life on Earth.

Universal Basic Income

Governments should provide everyone with enough money to live on. We should end poverty, hunger and homelessness, these horrors are needless and unjustifiable.

With a universal basic income, we would break the relationship between work and worth. We would be supporting the people (mostly women) on whose unpaid labour our societies currently depend. People could focus on doing the things they felt were important or necessary for themselves and their communities. We would start valuing people as living beings primarily rather than as economic units. It would be a good and simple move to help us shift away from exploitative consumerism and towards sustainability.

If people were not obliged to work for money, more people would grow their own food, cook from scratch and make the things they need. More people would dabble in small scale production, which is far more sustainable. We might have to pay more to get people doing the most essential jobs. At the moment, we depend on fear of abject poverty to provide us with front line workers. UBI would end exploitative workplaces and would require companies to treat employees with care and respect. The intrinsic values of jobs would become more important and people would focus on job satisfaction more than on money. We'd no doubt see radical shifts in employment and the kinds of businesses that could even exist, and that would all be to the good.

Four Day Working Weeks

Shorter working weeks for the same money tend to result in better productivity. That means having the mental resources to think more effectively about what you're doing. We could do without the environmental costs of make-work, and of the wastes of energy and resources that are inevitable when people are tired and stressed. Allowing people to be people rather than demanding they be machines would move us towards wiser and kinder working environments. It would be part of the essential slowing down process, reducing commuting and sharing out work more fairly.

Radical Changes to Agriculture

Where people are able to get on the land, dramatic changes can be made to reduce the harm caused by factory farming animals, and the harm caused by big monocultures – usually grains. We need a serious collective look at land use, and land access, and this really is going to need government support and leadership.

Food is both our most essential industry and one of our major sources of carbon. At the same time, the way land is managed by big businesses has a huge impact on biodiversity, water health, soil health, human health and human access to the landscape. Human bodies need access to dirt, human minds need green spaces. Most of us are totally alienated from food production and urban lifestyles can leave us feeling disconnected.

We could have kinder approaches to farming that takes better care of wild and domestic beings alike. We could do that in a way that includes more people, and produces healthier, safer food for people. We could safeguard waterways, fight desertification, deal with flooding and erosion and all those other landscape issues exacerbated by climate change.

You can get more food from an area of land if you are producing a diverse array of fruit and veg, with some animal inclusion. This leads to a healthier diet for people. Grain monocultures cause more problems than they solve in terms of human health, soil health and planet health.

We would all benefit from more time in green spaces. People going 'away' in search of pristine nature just put more pressure on our wild spaces. If we grew food in a way that nourished all aspects of human life while taking better care of the environment, we could do so much to improve our lives and the health of the planet itself.

In the UK we need to outlaw grouse moors, and the burning of grouse moors. We need to rewild the enormous stretches of land that are being misused in this way.

Reducing Waste

Why is there anything you can buy that cannot be re-used or re-cycled easily? Why do we have throw-away things that do not biodegrade safely in short time frames? The only reason is to protect the profits of companies. Meanwhile we pay to have our waste collected by our councils, and we pay environmentally if it ends up in landfill or an incinerator.

Much of what we buy is overpackaged in containers that will either go to landfill, or be shipped abroad after use, all too often to cause massive environmental problems somewhere else instead. Affluent countries are getting rather too good at outsourcing both production and waste disposal, while complaining about the carbon footprints of the countries who are doing our dirty work.

We could change the terms on which companies are allowed to send material to landfill. In 2021 it came to light that Amazon were in the habit of simply throwing away perfectly usable technology if it struck the company as financially advantageous to do so. That kind of action could simply be outlawed. We could require companies to account for their waste and take responsibility for it. We could go further and make companies responsible for their output after what they do becomes unusable – which would also solve the problem of built in obsolescence, non-reusable and non-recyclable components.

It's not enough to simply replace packaging with recyclable packaging. We use too much material. Swapping single use plastics for single use cardboard would just create a different set of problems and still uses up too many resources. We need a total rethink on how we do packaging and how we move things around. We can't afford most single use items and we need to move away from them entirely as a concept. While we're doing that, we need to keep an eye out for ableism. Plastic straws are a good case in point here – most of us don't need straws at all and can certainly do without single use ones. For some disabled people, disposable straws are really helpful and enabling and there are complications around swapping in more durable ones.

Stop Making Money out of Money

The thing about making money out of money is that no one else benefits. Often, it piles on the harm. At the moment, limited companies are under a legal obligation to grow profits for shareholders. That pressure for eternal growth is a driving force in rampant consumerism and we'd be much better off without it. Shareholder profit adds to the pressure to exploit workers and the natural world alike.

I'm not a fan of landlords. The cost of renting puts many working people in perpetually unstable and financially perilous situations. Even worse than this are the people and companies buying property as investment, and then just leaving it empty and unusable. This creates scarcity, drives up rental prices, and creates eyesores and holes in towns and cities. There are ways of using it as a tax dodge, and when scarcity of land drives up prices, a profit can be made from keeping something out of viable use. This also increases the push to use greenfield sites.

People who make money out of money aren't doing useful work or contributing to their communities through their efforts. The whole process is parasitic. Any enterprise that enables people to profit from the labour of others while making no contribution themselves should, in my opinion, be outlawed.

As a related issue, we need to do away with state sponsored capitalism. Companies should be held to account internationally so that the tax avoidance of the richest becomes impossible. Companies should not be able to get state funding if they are passing on dividends to shareholders. All too often, profit is privatised while risk is publicly owned and that has to change. Essential things should not be run for profit – health, education, infrastructure and policing should not be viewed as profit-making activities. Privately owned prisons are an obscenity.

As it stands, much of the world now has land ownership systems that are based on historic violence. Land that used to belong to the people living on it now doesn't, and violence is always involved in that kind of theft. We should be asking serious questions about who owns land and on what terms, how much land a person or company can fairly own and how much historic injustice can be tackled by land redistribution. Inheriting land that was taken from its original inhabitants by force is not an ethically acceptable basis for wealth.

Pollution and Ecocide

Pollution and ecocide know no boundaries. The Earth is full of diverse ecosystems, but our key life support systems are international. The state of our oceans is critical for our wellbeing, and we are devastating them. Climate is an international issue, and destruction in one part of the world hurts everyone. We're dealing with resources that are finite on a global scale. Air pollution impacts on everyone. Greenhouse gases are not a local issue. Our best hope of making real change lies in getting our cowardly world leaders to square up to these facts and act swiftly.

Ecocide is a key contempt missing from international law. It should be illegal to act in a way that harms the planet. Of course, many industries simply wouldn't be viable if they were told that planet-killing activities must cease. It is a very special kind of madness to put profits ahead of our viability as a species.

Business as usual is killing us. We have to change – individually, and internationally. Time is running out. To be real and present in the anthropocene means facing this and acting accordingly. We have to change, and demand change.

Not Just Changing the Technology

We can't just make the technology greener and carry on as we are. We can't replace fossil fuel powered cars with electric ones and keep on building roads and sitting in traffic queues. We can't replace single use plastic with single use cardboard. Robot bees are not the answer. Genetically modified crops are not the answer. More efficient gadgets will not make it feasible for everyone to have ever more gadgets. Farming innovations will not make it sustainable for everyone to eat large quantities of factory farmed meat.

We have to accept that the consumerist dream is a nightmare and that the things we've been taught to want are lethal for us. We have to scale back, use less and make much fewer demands on the planet. We have to stop putting carbon into the air and take radical steps to start sequestering it back in the natural world where it belongs. Carbon belongs in the ground, in trees and bogs, undamaged soil systems in untouched peat. It also belongs in the oceans, in the kelp beds, and the plankton. We've wreaked so much havoc on the restorative systems that were inherent on the planet that we're going to have to work hard to fix that.

We urgently need to share resources more equitably. We also need to work responsibly to curb human populations. It is the poorest and most vulnerable people around the world who are most likely to be killed by climate chaos. No one should see that as acceptable or as a way of reducing human impact.

Contraceptives should be freely available to everyone. Sexual education is a global necessity. Where women are empowered and enabled to control their family sizes, most will choose to do that. No one should have to depend on producing children to ensure their care and security in old age. Anyone who wishes to be sterilised should be allowed to go ahead with that. No woman should be denied sterilisation on the grounds that her husband – real or imagined – wants or might want children. Reducing population can be approached from a basis of empowering people – women in particular, allowing body autonomy and making it easier not to have children.

Culturally we can support this by not putting pressure on other people to have children. Don't criticise childless people or even ask them when they intend to reproduce. Don't criticise people for only having one child. Don't tell people who don't want children that they will regret it when they are older. Don't centre female identity around motherhood or perpetuate any ideas that reproduction is what women are for. If you want grandchildren, don't put pressure on your children to provide them – adopt. There are plenty of families out there who could use extra support from caring adults. Accept that no one is owed children, or grandchildren.

If you are part of a society that has structured itself around the idea of the nuclear family, work to challenge that. Humans are communal creatures, most of us don't like to live alone. Sexual reproduction is not the only basis for forming a household. Having your own children is not the only way to have a meaningful family life. Support diversity, and support the people who don't want to bear or raise children.

If you are part of a society that sees larger families as a status symbol, challenge it. This can be a religious issue, or about the display of wealth. Keeping a woman pregnant is also a popular choice with domestic abusers. Cultures that primarily treat women as wombs with legs perpetuate sexism, oppression and the abuse of women.

Take Action!

Change your life. Cut your carbon footprint. Don't wait for someone to provide leadership, make whatever changes you can. Pick the changes that will be easiest for you and do those first. Get into the habit of thinking about your life, questioning your desires and paying attention to what actually gives you meaning, richness and value.

Take action right now, and keep taking action because it is in your interests to do so. You can improve your quality of life with more authentic living choices. You are not here to be a cog in someone else's machine. Your existence should not be centred around making profits for other people. You are not here simply to work, consume, and die.

The biggest problems are not the fault of the majority of people living on this planet. Private jets, cruise ships, and SUVs are unsustainable, but few can afford them. Most of us can make a difference when it comes to our clothing choices. Anyone not living at the margins can probably cut down on waste and reduce their consumption of animal products. Eating less beef is a meaningful choice. What we can all do, is contribute to changing our culture. We need to stop celebrating over-consumption, greed and excessive wealth. We need to focus on kinder and more life-celebrating ways of being in the world.

We urgently need to change the stories that dominate our cultures. We need to think about real worth and real value, not just money and shiny tat. The quest for a good quality of life for ourselves, and for everyone else is entirely compatible with a push towards viable living. The unsustainable things that humans do cost us far more than we gain, and so many of those gains only exist in our minds because of how we imagine their social significance. Without health, relationships and peace, affluence isn't worth much at all.

About the Author

I have written a number of titles for Moon Books – *Druidry and Meditation, Druidry and the Ancestors, When a Pagan Prays, Spirituality without Structure,* and *Pagan Dreaming.* I also edited the anthology *Pagan Planet* and have contributed to other Moon Books anthologies.

As a Druid, I've spent my adult life trying to live lightly. There's a great deal to learn about what is possible, and what's effective, and this is always a work in progress and never as good as I want it to be. I feel very strongly about the need for real change and quietly rage about greenwashing and the ridiculousness of 'offsetting'. Harm cannot be offset.

I have benefited considerably from contact with the Transition Towns Network, and must particularly thank Erik in that regard for his ongoing support. I've been involved with many charities and organisations along the way, and I read a lot of books. This isn't a proper bibliography, but a few books I recommend for further and deeper reading.

Doughnut Economics - Kate Raworth
Enough is Plenty - Anne B. Ryan
From What Is to What If - Rob Hopkins
Healthy Planet - Fred Hageneder
Ecolinguistics - Arran Stibbe

MOON
BOOKS

PAGANISM & SHAMANISM

What is Paganism? A religion, a spirituality, an alternative belief system, nature worship? You can find support for all these definitions (and many more) in dictionaries, encyclopaedias, and text books of religion, but subscribe to any one and the truth will evade you. Above all Paganism is a creative pursuit, an encounter with reality, an exploration of meaning and an expression of the soul. Druids, Heathens, Wiccans and others, all contribute their insights and literary riches to the Pagan tradition. Moon Books invites you to begin or to deepen your own encounter, right here, right now.

If you have enjoyed this book, why not tell other readers by posting a review on your preferred book site.

Other books in the *Earth Spirit* series

Belonging to the Earth
Nature Spirituality in a Changing World
Julie Brett
978-1-78904-969-5 (Paperback)
978-1-78904-970-1 (ebook)

Confronting the Crisis
Essays and Meditations on Eco-Spirituality
David Sparenberg
978-1-78904-973-2 (Paperback)
978-1-78904-974-9 (ebook)

Eco-Spirituality and Human–Animal Relationships
Through an Ethical and Spiritual Lens
Mark Hawthorne
978-1-78535-248-5 (Paperback)
978-1-78535-249-2 (ebook)

Healthy Planet
Global Meltdown or Global Healing
Fred Hageneder
978-1-78904-830-8 (Paperback)
978-1-78904-831-5 (ebook)

Honoring the Wild
Reclaiming Witchcraft and Environmental Activism
Irisanya Moon
978-1-78904-961-9 (Paperback)
978-1-78904-962-6 (ebook)

Saving Mother Ocean
We all need to help save the seas!
Steve Andrews
978-1-78904-965-7 (Paperback)
978-1-78904-966-4 (ebook)

The Circle of Life is Broken
An Eco-Spiritual Philosophy of the Climate Crisis
Brendan Myers
978-1-78904-977-0 (Paperback)
978-1-78904-978-7 (ebook)

Readers of ebooks can buy or view any of these bestsellers by
clicking on the live link in the title. Most titles are published in
paperback and as an ebook. Paperbacks are available in traditional
bookshops. Both print and ebook formats are available online.

Find more titles and sign up to our readers' newsletter at
http://www.johnhuntpublishing.com/paganism
Follow us on Facebook at https://www.facebook.com/MoonBooks
and Twitter at https://twitter.com/MoonBooksJHP